RELATIVES

Owing to the antiquity and rarity of this book, certain pages are regrettably absent, and readability is compromised due to the blurring of the original text. If you possess any insights regarding the availability of these missing sections, kindly inform us. Your assistance is crucial in ensuring the completion of this significant work for the benefit of future generations.

RELATIVES

BEING FURTHER VERSES TRANSLATED FROM THE SANSKRIT

BY

ARTHUR WILLIAM RYDER

GYAN

Published by

Gyan Publishing House
5, Ansari Road
Daryaganj, New Delhi-110002
Phone: 011-47034999, 9811692060
E-mail: books@gyanbooks.com

Distribution Network
gyanbooks.com
India, USA, Canada, UK, Australia

ISBN: 978-93-6280-309-2 (PB)
First Published, 1919

2nd Impression 2024

Printed at: Gyan Press, Delhi.

RELATIVES
Translator: ARTHUR WILLIAM RYDER

RELATIVES

BEING FURTHER VERSES TRANSLATED
FROM THE SANSKRIT

BY

ARTHUR WILLIAM RYDER

TRANSLATOR OF

Women's Eyes : Kalidasa : The Little Clay Cart : Twenty-Two Goblins

For a self-conceited modish life, made up of trifles, clinging to a corporeal civilization, hating ideas, there is no remedy like the Oriental largeness.—EMERSON.

SAN FRANCISCO
A. M. ROBERTSON
MCMXIX

TO MY FRIEND

LEON JOSIAH RICHARDSON

DIRECTOR, MILITARY BUREAU

UNIVERSITY OF CALIFORNIA

Six things are done by friends:
To take, and give again;
To listen, and to talk;
To dine, to entertain.

From the PANCHATANTRA

INTRODUCTION

This volume is in some sense a sequel to the poems from the Sanskrit presented under the title "Women's Eyes".

The present collection has less unity. Almost all of the verses of "Women's Eyes" were translated from Bhartrihari, the greatest Indian writer of verse epigrams. The verses here presented are from many sources, and the selections are of very different length and date. The only bond of union is this—that these poems are all taken from the ancient Sanskrit language, and all seemed to the translator worthy of an English rendering.

The oldest selection is the satirical Hymn to Faith, which is found in the Rigveda, and may have been composed more than a thousand years before the beginning of the Christian era. The latest is the Thief's Song, written in Kashmir in the eleventh century A. D. There are selections from Mahabharata and Ramayana, the two great epics whose beginnings precede by centuries the birth of Christ. There are poems by Bhartrihari and Kalidasa, poets for whom the date 500 A.D. is convenient, though probably only approximate. There are bits from the two fable books, Hitopadesha and Panchatantra, whose material is much more ancient than their present form.

I have striven faithfully for a literal rendering. Though a rendering into verse cannot be quite as close as a prose version, there are, in the shorter pieces and in the Thief's Song, no wilful additions or subtractions. In the longer narrative selections some condensation seemed desirable; here, too, nothing is added.

I am under obligations to the University of California Chronicle for permission to reprint certain verses which first appeared in its pages.

ARTHUR W. RYDER

BERKELEY, CALIFORNIA
September 20, 1919

CONTENTS

CONTENTS

CONTENTS

RELATIVES

From the RAMAYANA

I saw some great, wild elephants who
  Were gathered in a ring;
They saw some men with a lassoo,
  And they began to sing:

"We fear no fire nor goad nor sling,
  Nor any man that lives;
We do not fear a single thing
  Except our relatives.

For relatives are selfish, mean,
  And always setting traps:
We understand what we have seen;
  Perhaps we know — PERHAPS.

Girls give us hopes, too often vain;
  Cows give us tallow grease;
Our relatives give us a pain;
  The clergy give us peace.

RELATIVES

A thirsty bee will kiss a flower,
  And then extract the honey;
A relative will praise your power,
  And carry off your money.

An elephant will bathe his skin,
  Then dust it till it's black;
A relative will praise his kin,
  And stab them in the back.

We fear no fire nor goad nor sling,
  Nor any man that lives;
We do not fear a single thing
  Except our relatives."

A RULE OF LIFE

From the HITOPADESHA

To wealth and wisdom give your days,
  Like one whom age and death would spare;
Yet hourly walk in righteous ways,
  As if Death had you by the hair.

THE PERVERSITY OF FATE

From the ANTHOLOGY

I see a dog, but not a stone;
I find a stone, the dog is flown;
If dog and stone at once I view,
The king's dog! Damn! What can I do?

THE SLAVE TO HER MASTER

From KALIDASA'S MALAVIKA

My love is all in vain;
  Bid hope depart,
  My heart!

Yet thrills in me again
  What will not bear
  Despair.

Beloved, give to me
  The joy unknown
  Alone;

For slavery keeps from thee,
  Lord of my life!
  Thy wife.

A FAITHFUL FRIEND

From KALIDASA'S MALAVIKA

To bring hard matters to an end,
One needs to have a faithful friend:
To see an object in the night,
Even eyes must have a candle's light.

A FAITHLESS FRIEND

From the PANCHATANTRA

Whoever trusts a faithless friend
And twice in him believes,
Lays hold on death as willingly
As when a mule conceives.

FRIENDSHIP'S BROTHERS

From the PANCHATANTRA

To give us birth we need a mother;
  For second birth we need another:
And friendship's brothers seem by far
  More dear than natural brothers are.

HEEDLESSNESS

From BHARTRIHARI

Old age, an awful tigress, growls:
And shafts of sickness pierce the bowels;
Life's water trickles from its jar—
'Tis strange how thoughtless people are.

OLD AGE

From Bhartrihari

Gone long ago are they who gave us birth;
Old friends are memories upon this earth;
Our lives are undermined and daily sink,
Like trees upon the river's sandy brink.

THE CHESS-GAME

From Bhartrihari

Where there were scattered pieces on the board,
There now is one;
Next, many slaughtered pieces are restored,
Then all are gone:
The dice are day and night; the board is life;
Time and again
Death plays a fearful chess-game with his wife —
The pawns are men.

MANU AND THE FISH

From the Mahabharata

I

There was a gentle, holy sage
Named Manu, in a former age.
The woes of life he would not blink;
For many years he did not wink.

With ragged clothes and frowsy hair
He lived beside a stream. And there
He saw a fish who thus began
To speak to him. "O holy man,

I am a little fish, you see;
And bigger fishes frighten me.
For bigger fishes eat the small;
It is their nature, once for all.

So dreadful terror weighs me down;
Besides, I fear that I shall drown.
Then save me. Some day I will do
An equal favor, sir, to you."

II

So Manu, when he heard his wish,
Stretched forth a hand, and took the fish,
And dropped him in a water-jar
That was as bright as moonbeams are.

And in the jar the little fish
Had everything his heart could wish.
He grew and thrived on food and fun,
For Manu loved him like a son.

At last he grew too big by far
To live within the water-jar.
He said: "Good Manu, I would thank
You very kindly for a tank."

So Manu took him to a tank
Eight miles in breadth from bank to bank,
And twice as long. There, free from fears,
He lived and grew for many years.

III

And when he grew too big to play
There in a comfortable way,
He said to Manu: "Pray deliver,
And put me in the Ganges River.

And I will never show you spite,
But some day help you, as is right.
My growth has not been selfish; it
Has happened for your benefit."

Kind Manu, anxious to deliver
His friend, went to the Ganges River,
And left him happy. As before
He grew in time a little more.

And then he said to Manu: "Dear,
I can no longer wiggle here.
My holy friend, be good to me,
And take me quickly to the sea."

So Manu took him tenderly
And travelled quickly to the sea.
The fish tried not to weigh too much,
And to be nice to smell and touch.

IV

The fish, when he had reached the ocean,
Smiled at his holy friend's devotion,
And said: "O kind and holy man,
You do as much as fathers can.

And now 'tis time for me to do
A little something, dear, for you.
For you must know, my holy friend,
The world is hastening to its end.

A dreadful time is near at hand
For all the things that move or stand;
There comes a flood that has no bound,
And everybody will be drowned.

So build a ship and build it strong:
Put ropes on board both stout and long.
And one thing further you will need,
Neat packages of every seed.

Embark then with the seven seers,
And wait, good Manu, free from fears,
Until I come. And you will see
A horn upon the head of me.

Till then, farewell. Do not delay.
The danger grows from day to day."

V

Then Manu packed most carefully
The seeds, and straightway put to sea.
His good ship gently rose and fell
Upon the ocean's mighty swell.

He longed to see the friendly fish,
Who came in answer to the wish.
He seemed a floating mountain dread;
A horn was growing on his head.

So Manu, feeling less forlorn,
Fastened a rope about the horn,
And felt the ship glide speedily
Over the dancing, salty sea.

But when the wind began to roar
And ocean thundered more and more,
The tossing, shaken ship began
To stagger like a drunken man.

No land remained to cheer them there,
But only water, sky, and air;
No life through all those many years
Save Manu, fish, and seven seers.

But Manu, all those many years,
Went sailing with the seven seers;
The fish pulled on with might and main
And did not weary nor complain.

At last he did, however, stop
Beside the highest mountain-top,
And bade them tie the ship; and they
Call it Ship Mountain to this day.

VI

And then, with wide, unwinking eyes,
The fish, to Manu's great surprise,
Declared: "I saved the seven seers
From death and agonizing fears;

For I am Brahma. And my friend,
Kind Manu, who has seen the end
Of all the world, shall make again
Gods, devils, animals, and men."

And so he disappeared. But they,
Amazed, departed on their way,
While kindly Manu made again
Gods, devils, animals, and men.

Now all have heard who had the wish
The tale of Manu and the fish.
And everyone who takes it in,
Shall be forever free from sin.

THOUGHTS ON HAVING ONE'S WIFE STOLEN BY A GIANT

From the RAMAYANA. This is the lament of the hero Rama, when his wife Sita is carried away by Ravan, the giant king of Ceylon.

They say that as the seasons move,
  Our sorrow gently fades away;
But I am far from her I love
  And sorrow deepens every day.

That she is gone, is not my woe;
  That she was reft, is not my pain;
The thought that agonizes so
  Is this; her youth is spent in vain.

Blow, breezes, blow to her dear face;
  Blow back to me her kisses sweet:
Through you we taste a glad embrace,
  And in the moon our glances meet.

When she was torn away from me,
  "My lord! My love!" was all her cry,
Which tortures me incessantly;
  My heart is poisoned, and I die.

RELATIVES

I burn upon an awful pyre;
  My body wastes by day and night;
Her loss is fuel to feed the fire
  That burns so pitilessly white.

If I could leave each loving friend,
  Could sink beneath the sea, and sleep,
Perhaps the fire of love would end,
  If I could slumber in the deep.

One thought consoles my worst distress;
  Through this I live: I cannot die
While she lies down in loveliness
  Upon the self-same earth as I.

The sun-parched rice, no longer wet,
  Lives on, while earth her moisture gives;
The root of love supports me yet,
  For they have told me that she lives.

Though giants hem her round, yet soon
  She shall be freed, and shall arise
As radiantly as the moon
  From clouds that darken autumn skies.

When shall I pierce the giant's breast
  With shafts that suck his life away,
That give my tortured darling rest
  And all her absent griefs allay?

When shall I feel the close embrace
  Of my good goddess, as in dreams?
When kiss her smile, while on her face
  The water born of gladness gleams?

When shall I pluck from out my heart—
  A heart by woes of absence torn—
The pain of life from love apart,
  Forget it, like a garment worn?

THE FORTUNATE FOOL

From Bhartrihari

God to the fool a way has shown,
A way unfailing, all his own,
To hide his lack of sense;
For each, however great a fool,
Among the wise may wear the jewel
Called Silence.

FORESIGHT

From Bhartrihari

From loving girls, ye wise, refrain;
'Tis little pleasure, longer pain.
But love three females none the less,
Compassion, Wisdom, Friendliness.
For swelling breasts of lovely girls,
Trembling beneath their strings of pearls,
And hips with jingling girdles — well,
They do not help you much in hell.

PROXIES

From the HITOPADESHA

When righteous acts must needs be done,
When time of service has begun,
    In caring for the servant crowd,
In the begetting of a son,
    No proxies are allowed.

A PRAYER

From BHARTRIHARI

O father wind, friend light, and earth my mother!
O kinsman water, heaven's space my brother!
    I bow, I pray: with you in union blest
May I be good, in brightest wisdom smother
    The dark, and sink at last in God to rest.

SIMPLE JUSTICE

From Amaru

If, maiden of the lotus eye,
  Your anger hurts you so,
'Tis right you should not let it die,
  You hardly could, you know.

But once I gave you an embrace,
  To keep it would be pain;
And once I kissed your willing face,
  Give me that kiss again.

ONE FATE OF TWO

From BHARTRIHARI

One fate of two for the jasmine flower,
  The same for the wise and good;
To shine at the head of all the world,
  Or to wither in the wood.

GENTLENESS

From the MAHABHARATA

To gentleness the ruffians bend,
  And gentlefolk no less;
It moves relentless to its end —
  So fierce is gentleness.

POT-EAR'S AWAKENING

From the RAMAYANA. When the giant citadel in Ceylon was invested by Rama and his army, the giant king determined to call to his assistance his most redoubtable subject, Pot-ear. This giant was normally awake only one day every six months. He must therefore be awakened before he can employ his great strength and courage in the giant cause.

I

They started forth, the giant band
Obedient to their king's command,
With flesh and blood as tempting food,
With wreaths and perfumes, sweet and good.

And so they came to Pot-ear's door,
Where stretched the cave a league and more
On every side, where blossoms sweet
Poured fragrance forth, a guest to greet.

And all that mighty giant band
Before his snoring scarce could stand;
They tottered, but with spirit brave
They fought their way into the cave.

There Pot-ear stretched this way and that
Just like a mountain tumbled flat,
Hideous in his slumber deep,
For he was very sound asleep.

They saw him bristle, saw him shake;
They heard him hissing like a snake;
They felt his breathing like a storm
That blew them from his ugly form.

They saw his nostrils sink and swell,
His throat that yawned like gates of hell;
The dreadful, sprawling form they saw
That smelt of dinners eaten raw.

They made a mountain of the food
That they had brought, so sweet and good;
Beside his bed the mountain rose
Of deer and boars and buffaloes.

They grasped their trumpets glittering bright
As moonbeams shining in the night;
Impatiently they blew and blew,
And screamed and howled and shouted, too.

Through all the tumult loud and deep
Pot-ear lay snoring, fast asleep;
They saw he did not mind their clamor
And seized a stone, or club, or hammer.

They tumbled boulders on his chest,
To see if they could break his rest.
They beat a hundred rub-a-dubs
With fists and hammers, bars and clubs.

The only answer was a snore
A little deeper than before
That blew away the giant band;
Before his breath they could not stand.

More sternly yet the giants strove:
With sticks and whips and goads they drove
Horses and elephants abreast,
Asses and camels on his chest.

They clubbed and pounded without pity,
Until the tumult filled the city;
They made the woods and mountains shake,
But giant Pot-ear would not wake.

Then anger filled each giant breast;
They swore that they would break his rest.
One last attack they made at length
With all their might and wrath and strength.

And there were some to beat the drum,
While screamed and howled and shouted some;
Some bit his ears, while some would tear
Away great handfuls of his hair.

A hundred water-pots they poured
Into his ears, and still he snored;
They could not shake his slumber deep;
Pot-ear was very sound asleep.

Some took a hammer or a club,
With all their might began to drub
Upon his chest and limbs and head
To wake him from his drowsy bed.

They tied great, spiky stones to ropes
And dragged them over him; their hopes
Were disappointed still; for he
Slept on with peaceful dignity.

But when a thousand elephants
Upon his chest began to dance,
Then Pot-ear, gently tickled, broke
From bonds of slumber, and awoke.

He did not heed the falling stones
Or clubs that rattled on his bones,
But yawned and raised himself to see
What breakfast might provided be.

The giants pointed to the food
That they had brought, so sweet and good;
Then Pot-ear in his might arose
And ate some boars and buffaloes.

II

Now when the meat, with wine afloat,
Had vanished down his mighty throat,
Dull Pot-ear shook his heavy head,
And rolled his sleepy eyes, and said:

"Great matters surely are at stake,
Or I should hardly be awake;
And for our giant king, I will
Cool fire or overturn a hill

But tell me why I am awake;
Surely great matters are at stake."
Then giant Post-eye bent him low
And humbly answered: "Pot-ear, know

That neither gods nor devils can
Affright us—but we fear a man.
He leads his mountainous apes across
The strait, for grief at Sita's loss.

One ape has burned our splendid town
And he has struck Prince Aksha down.
While Ravan, heaven's scourge and thorn,
Has been by Rama overborne

In single fight, and has been spared—
A thing no god or devil dared."
Then Pot-ear rolled his eyes, and said:
"Well, I will strike the monkeys dead,

With Lakshman and with Rama, and
Before our king as victor stand.
And monkey flesh and blood shall be
Your food — the blood of men for me."

So Pot-ear, rising, took a cup
And drank, to keep his courage up;
He drank two thousand jars of wine,
And washed his face, and made it shine.

Eager, excited, haughty, proud,
He towered above the giant crowd;
And as he strode his king to greet,
Earth trembled underneath his feet.

III

On, to his brother's proud abode,
Half-drunk with sleep and wine, he strode;
Red-eyed with wrath, he bowed him low,
And asked; "Why was I wakened so?

What danger threatens, or what ill?
Whom would you like to have me kill?"
And Ravan, maddened by his wrong,
Said: "Brother, you have slept too long;

So all the wickedness and woe
That Rama works, you do not know;
How he has built a bridge, and crossed
The channel with a monkey host.

Behold their strangely hideous shapes!
See Lanka's groves, one sea of apes!
They kill our bravest when we fight;
For who can conquer monkey might?

Ah, brother, save your stricken nation,
Your king reduced to supplication;
You know I love you and adore you;
I know how devils flee before you.

So, if you have a warrior's might,
Or if you love your brother, fight!
Or if you would not sulk apart
While trouble makes me sad at heart.

He only is a friend indeed
Who aids his sinful friend in need,
Who indefatigably gives
A helping hand to relatives."

IV

Then Pot-ear felt his brother's woe,
And answered softly, soothing, slow:
"In battle's forefront I will slay
Rama, and chase his apes away.

Yes, I would drink the sea, eat fire,
Slay Death himself, should you desire;
Would crush the mountains, pierce the earth,
Smite sun and stars, to bring you mirth,

And food to me. I sleep so long
And grow so hungry and so strong
That earth and heaven and hell would be
A not too bounteous meal for me.

Rejoice, and let your heart incline
To every pleasure rare and fine,
And murmur, as you sip your wine:
'Sita is mine, forever mine'."

V

So Ravan, knowing Pot-ear's might,
Rejoiced, and felt his heart grow light;
While Pot-ear grasped, his foe to strike,
His trusty, gold-bespangled pike —

The pike that gods and devils feared,
Made of black iron, in spots besmeared
With many a stain and blotch of red,
By foemen's blood contributed.

Then, maddened by the reek of blood,
To the great city wall he strode,
While flowers and prayers upon him fell,
And drums and trumpets wished him well.

And there he paused and spoke: "To-day
Shall all the monkeys fade away
Like moths in flame. I would not care
To hurt them in their forest lair;

Indeed, the species often proves
Quite ornamental in our groves;
But Rama is the cause of all
Our woe; so he and his must fall."

He spoke, nor heeded signs of ill
That waited on his footsteps still—
The sky as red as asses' skin,
The clouds with lightning mingled in,

The jackals spitting fire on high,
The throbbing arm, the twitching eye,
The vulture on his pike-staff croaking,
The thunderbolt before him smoking.

He heeded not, but leaped the wall,
Obeying thus the certain call
Of Death; and straight the monkey crowds
Scattered and fled like riven clouds.

But Angad called: "Why would you flee
Like apes of mean or no degree?
Return and prove your valor: thus
He shall not prove a match for us."

Ashamed, they seized upon great boulders
Or lifted trees upon their shoulders;
The trees were splintered, striking him;
Rocks split upon his every limb.

While underneath his blows they bled
And swooned and died, or turned and fled;
Till Angad called them back to fight,
Reproving thus their shameless flight:

"Why save your lives? Why run away?
What will the monkey women say?
For high-born monkeys may not flee
Like vulgar apes of no degree.

And if we fight our best and die,
We win a hero's home on high;
If victory should crown our worth,
We win a hero's name on earth.

"But life is dear to us:" they said,
"And Pot-ear quickly strikes us dead."
Yet, rallying to their prince's name,
They fought once more for very shame.

VI

They sought for courage in despair:
For wounds and death they did not care
Nor for their scores and hundreds slain
And eaten on the battle-plain.

Then great Hanuman hurled a shower
Of boulders, using all his power;
But Pot-ear answered with a blow
From that fierce pike, that laid him low.

The mountain crag that Nila hurled
He caught, as through the air it whirled,
And powdered it, till sparks and flame
Forth from the tortured missile came.

Then monkeys by the thousand poured
Upon him, bit and tore and roared;
Even as they clawed and gashed and smote,
They vanished in their hell, his throat.

"With Rama only will I fight,"
Cried Pot-ear: "then will put to flight,
When he is dead, your warriors all;"
And Rama answered Pot-ear's call

With shafts that pierced his shaggy chest;
Then, spitting fire, with bleeding breast,
He charged, but from his weakened hand
The weapons dropped upon the sand.

Yet with bare, weakened hands he slew
Two hundred monkeys as they flew
Upon him; then, with tempest-shock
He hurled a craggy, ponderous rock

At Rama, who evaded it,
While Pot-ear, in a foaming fit,
Turned, licking bloody chops, and slew
Of monkey warriors not a few.

And hoarsely laughing, shouted so:
"Rama, I am no common foe
Like those that you have slain; this club
With which I have been wont to drub

The gods and devils, you shall feel
As it prepares you for my meal."
An answering arrow cut away
The right arm and the club. They lay

Immense. A second arrow sped
And shore away his bleeding head,
Which tumbled, grinning horribly,
Among the fishes in the sea.

Then choirs of heaven praised the might
Of Rama in that dreadful fight;
And monkey faces blossomed bright
Like lilies in the glad sun-light.

VII

But in the city Ravan kept
A tortured vigil, moaned and wept:

"Ah, Pot-ear! Source of all my hope and gladness!
Where are you flown,
Leaving unplucked your brother's thorn of sadness,
Dying alone?

My right arm were you; you I trusted only,
Death's match! And can
The tamer of high gods be sleeping lonely,
Slain by a man?

The gods rejoice, forgetting all their anguish;
Foes not a few
Soon will assail the fortress where I languish,
Grieving for you.

I am no king, nor Sita's lover longer—
Till I shall give
Battle to Rama, prove myself the stronger,
Vainly I live.

And should it be his lot to slay another,
Gladly I die;
Beside the headless form that was my brother,
There let me lie."

FORTITUDE

From the MAHABHARATA. This is the consolation offered to those who have lost kinsmen in the great epic war.

All gathering ends in dissipation;
All heaps, at last, must fall;
All friendships melt in separation;
And death at last ends all.

The coward dies, the hero lives
A space, but none pass by
The appointed days that heaven gives—
Then let us fighting die.

All lives begin from nothingness,
Stir for a time, and then
(No cause for grief) sink into less
Than nothingness again.

Death has no enemy nor friend;
Each in his turn must pass,
Must helpless to that bidding bend
As wind-blown blades of grass.

Our goal is — there. And every day
 The one long caravan
Moves on with death to point the way.
 Why should it grieve a man?

For all the saints and scholars old
 Since first the world began
Are gone, with every fighter bold.
 Why should it grieve a man?

The fighter slain attains to heaven;
 The other wins the fight;
To each is much advantage given;
 Fighting is good and right.

And God, who loves a fighting man,
 Hailing a welcome guest,
Prepares with all the care he can,
 A seat among the blest.

Oh, trust yourself, and spare your tears
 For those who fell in strife;
Not all your sorrow, pain, and fears
 Can bring the dead to life.

RELATIVES

Hundreds of parents, sons, and wives
  Loved you with passion true;
Gone are the loves of former lives—
  What do they mean to you?

Time makes us win our strength, and keep;
  Time tells us when to die;
Time is awake when others sleep;
  Time passes no man by.

Youth vanishes, and beauty, wealth,
  And love and friendship die
With life itself and living health;
  But wise men do not cry.

They do not cry, but fight; and then
  Forget their former woes;
For pain forgotten is not pain,
  But pain remembered, grows.

This wisdom heals the heart's dull woes
  As herbs the body's pain;
When palliating wisdom grows,
  We are not children then.

One thing remains of all our loves,
  Our wealth and honors won —
The character that onward moves,
  The deeds that we have done.

Man has no enemy nor friend
  Except himself; alone
He knows what deeds to virtue tend,
  What seeds of sin are sown

HYMN TO FAITH

From the RIGVEDA

By Faith the holy fire is lit,
  And sung the liturgy;
We pray to Faith with all our wit
  For prosperous piety.

Give wealth, O Faith, to me who give
  Such worship as I can;
Make me respected, make me live
  A rich, religious man.

The gods have faith from imps, I see;
  For what they will, they can;
Enlarge my prosperous piety
  As a rich, religious man.

Gods worship Faith, and pious men
  Must worship every hour;
If faith first fills our bosoms, then
  Faith gives us wealth and power.

We call on Faith by morning's light,
  On Faith in glare of day,
On Faith when evening sinks to night:
  O Faith, give faith to pray!

WIPE OUT DELUSION

From Bhartrihari

Wipe out delusion, O my soul!
  Seek peace in Shiva ever;
Dwell on the banks whereunder roll
  Floods of the sacred river;

Who trusts in waves that break and crash,
  In bonfires' flaming flakes,
In bubble or in lightning-flash,
  In women, streams, or snakes?

LIFE

From Bhartrihari

Here is the sound of lutes, and there are screams and wailing;
Here winsome girls, there bodies old and failing;
Here scholars' talk, there drunkards' mad commotion —
Is life a nectared or a poisoned potion?

HOW LONG, O LORD?

From Bhartrihari

Alone, without desire, at rest,
In atmosphere of heaven drest,
My hand for spoon, when shall I be,
O Shiva, God! from *karma* free?

LITERARY CRITICISM

From KALIDASA'S MALAVIKA

Established fame is not enough;
Not all the new is wretched stuff.
The wise approve where'er they may;
The fools repeat what critics say.

A JOY FOREVER

From BHARTRIHARI

The poet-kings who know the art
To touch the chord that moves the heart,
  Secure may draw their breath;
Far from the body of their fame apart
  Lurk fears of age and death.

HOSPITALITY

From the HITOPADESHA

A mat of straw upon the floor,
  Water, and kindly words as well:
These things at least, if nothing more,
  Are always found where good men dwell.

HE CAN'T STAND PROSPERITY

From the MAHABHARATA

The man who does not steel his heart
  To evil fates and fair,
Is crumbled by prosperity
  Like unbaked earthenware.

NO NEED OF BOASTING

From the MAHABHARATA

The wise who conquer cities vast,
  Win wealth untold, and call
The mighty earth their own, are not
  Disposed to boast at all.

The fire cooks silently; the sun
  Shines, but he does not talk;
The dumb earth bears all moving things
  And all that do not walk

DRONA'S DEATH

From the MAHABHARATA. Drona is the eighty-year old hero who had instructed the heroes of both the opposing armies in the use of arms.

While Drona led the Kuru van,
The Pandu army to a man
Was beaten back and strove in vain
To dominate the battle-plain.

Where tramp and clash of battle grew
Like crackling flames in dry bamboo,
There Drona blazed, a smokeless fire
That fed on death and mounted higher.

Where aged Drona's arrows passed,
Horse, man, and tusker breathed their last.
Like hissing snakes his arrows sped
And left a trail of reeking red.

The Pandu army fought in vain
Against him. They had all been slain,
Had not they striven to beguile
Their foe with false and wicked wile.

For Bhima cried aloud and said:
"Old man, your son is stark and dead.

As silly simpletons will fight
For wife and child and money bright,
So you have fought—and all for one,
Your dearly loved, your only son;

Who studied in the school of strife,
And paid his lesson with his life.
Dead on the plain his body lies
A prey to all that creeps and flies."

The father heard the lie, and slow
His hand released the fatal bow;
He sank, yet roused himself again
In one strong cry: "Fight on, my men!

Destroy the treacherous Pandu line,
But hope no more for aid of mine.
All hatred dies from out my breast;
Remains religion's peaceful rest."

His foe believed the Brahman's word
And darted with uplifted sword
To pierce him through, while all the men
And all the horses shrieked in pain.

But Drona, in ecstatic prayer,
Knew not his foe was standing there;
Wrapped in inviolable fire,
He thought on God with pure desire.

We saw his lifted face; we heard
His murmuring lips pronounce the word
"Amen!" We felt him pray; at last
We knew his hero soul had passed.

For while his body tumbled dead,
A flame flashed from his cloven head;
His soul flew in the flame above
To dwell with God in deathless love.

There were but five of mortal birth
Who saw his spirit leave the earth;
Who heard the choirs of angels sing
Divinely in their welcoming;

Saw heaven's everlasting fire
Flash out, and flicker, and expire;
And knew that he was with the saints
Where God's love wearies not nor faints.

But all could see the bloody corse,
By arrows torn and trampling horse;
All sorrowed for the evil done
Save one insatiate foe alone,

Who scorned our hero's eighty years
And scant hair gray behind the ears;
He hacked the body from the head,
To show his hatred for the dead.

And all the army fled away;
Where Drona died, they could not stay;
But Drona's spirit dwells on high
Among the stars that light the sky.

THE THIRSTY FOOL

From the KATHASARITSAGARA

A thirsty fool had labored much
  To reach a river fair;
Then would not drink, perceiving such
  A lot of water there.

"Why do n't you drink?" A neighbor cried
  Who saw the thing befall;
"How can I?" Simpleton replied;
  "I could n't drink it all."

"Suppose you leave a little bit,"
  Said neighbor, "Do you think
The king would punish you for it?"
  The booby would not drink.

Just like a fool! He sees a thing
  That terrifies his heart;
He loses time in dallying,
  And never gets a start.

PESSIMISM

From the MAHABHARATA

Our happiness is past; a curse
  On sin and lack of truth!
Yet each tomorrow will be worse,
  For earth has lost her youth.

Fraud and illusion crowd the time;
  Conduct and virtue flee;
Religion seeks a happier clime —
  The worst is yet to be.

OPTIMISM

From the RAMAYANA

Toward Death we move with every breath;
Death dogs us every day;
However far we journey, Death
Is never far away.

We laugh to see the rising sun,
And laugh to see him set;
Nor think that when the day is done,
Our days are fewer yet.

Our hearts are warm to each new spring,
Each summer, winter, fall;
But what the passing seasons bring
Is only Death to all.

As log collides with log upon
The sea, and parts again,
So friend and gold and wife and son
Love and abandon men.

RELATIVES

As if a traveler should meet
  A hurrying caravan,
And say: "I too with willing feet
  Will follow as I can,"

So to the long parade we cleave
  That with the world began:
Then do not grieve, you cannot leave
  The social caravan.

The hours of youth grow ever less;
  No river climbs the hill;
Then turn your thoughts to happiness,
  Which is your portion still.

THE THIEF'S SONG

The CHAURA-PANCHASHIKA of the poet Bilhana, who lived in Kashmir in the eleventh century. The thief has stolen a princess' heart, and has been thrown into prison, on the discovery of the intrigue, by the irate father. While awaiting the king's pleasure, he writes his song, which comes to the royal ear, procuring him liberty and the legitimation of his love. The verbal trick of the translation is found also in the Sanskrit.

As then she was, I think of her today:
  The face that blossomed as she woke from sleep,
The slender waist, the golden champaks gay,
  The self-surrendering love; and I must weep
  For magic happiness I could not keep.

If I could see her once again today,
  Fair as the moon, as beautifully pale,
Full-bosomed, love-sick, bearing queenly sway
  O'er youth and charm, that only would avail
  To heal my fever, and to make me hale.

If I could see her lotus-eyes today,
  The breast that into sloping shoulders slips,
Would I not clasp her in my arms straightway
  And drink the maddening honey of her lips,
  Drunk like the bee that from the lotus sips!

In prison I remember her today:
  Dark curls against the pallor of her cheek;
The soft resistance as she strove to stay
  My eager love with arms around my neck —
  Yet shamed, and even in her resisting, meek.

Awaiting death, I think of her today:
  Of her sweet face, her timid, downward glance,
Her eyes that in their restlessness betray
  The madness of love's long and waking trance —
  Queen-swan among love's flowering lily-plants!

If I could see her in my cell today,
  If arms that yearn for her could but receive her,
My best of love should comfort her, should slay
  The absence and the sorrows that bereave her,
  I'd close my eyes, and never, never leave her.

A vision comes to comfort me today,
  A slender form that gives to dance a grace
Unknown before with beauties that obey
  Love's bidding, and a pale but shining face,
  And earrings that in air strange patterns trace.

And I remember in my bonds today,
  How she, with soft, smooth sandal powder sweet,
And musk diffusing pungent perfume, lay
  Upon her couch, how arching brows would greet
  Her lovely eyes, like lips that kissing meet.

Here, chained and fettered, I recall today,
  The slender form, eyes veiled in modest fear,
The wine-sweet lips I kissed in loving play,
  The musk, the saffron of my own Kashmir,
  Betel, and camphor, that to her were dear

The crowning moment I recall today,
  When all her soul is given to my lips,
When, clad in love's warm, golden, glad array,
  My darling from the hated palace slips,
  Like to the moon delivered from eclipse.

But slighter joys are in my mind today,
  How once a lovers' quarrel checked our glee;
Then when I sneezed, the princess would not say
  "God bless you!" but with silent coquetry
  Stuck blossoms in her hair, to madden me.

RELATIVES

Another picture visits me today:
  The drops of weariness that oft would seek
To make upon her face a pearl inlay
  When love had left her pale and worn and weak;
  The golden earring that would fret her cheek.

I seem to see her lovely breast today,
  The skirt that tripped her quick steps on the floor,
The glance that modesty would lead astray
  And love bring back to me, the lips grown sore
  Because I would be kissing evermore.

I seem to see my princess-bride today
  Moving with swan-like, undulating grace,
And in her hand a red ashoka-spray,
  Pearl necklace on her breast in close embrace,
  Quick smiles that light the pallor of her face.

I see her gold-bespangled dress today
  Held as a frail defending shield, the pain
Of my too eager passion to allay,
  Clutched tightly as she struggles once again
  For very shame to leave me — but in vain.

RELATIVES

Her golden bracelets haunt my thoughts today,
  Her restless eyes that pierce a gloom like this
As memories that none can take away,
  The teeth of pearl, red lips, the secret bliss,
  The wealth of hair that fresh-picked blossoms kiss.

That wealth of hair I seem to see today
  When ribbons break and flowers begin to fall;
Then heaven is opened in the dazzling ray
  Of her dear smile; at love's imperious call
  We sink in bliss that none may share at all.

And I remember in my cell today
  How she would come to find me through the night,
Guided by beams illumining her way
  From lamps that glitter with a gem-like light
  On her shamed face, and mine with kindness bright.

Well I remember thee, my love, today:
  Thy startled eyes as of a gentle deer,
Thy body wasting at the least delay
  Of love, thy graceful gait, thy teeth so dear —
  Delights of heaven transplanted to Kashmir!

RELATIVES

I hear the echo of thy laugh today:
  I see thy bosom quiver in sheer glee;
I see the necklace, darting beams that stray
  About thy neck; sure, Love has planted thee
  Upon a hill, his bright flower flag to be!

Yes, I can hear through dungeon-walls today
  Sweet flatteries of thine, when, soon or late,
Passion grew weary in its house of clay;
  I hear the parrot quaintly imitate,
  Learning soft words to utter to her mate.

Even as in prison I recall today
  The limp, surrendered form, the luscious hair,
The half-shut eyes, the swanlike, queenly play
  In love's bright lotus-pool, I cannot bear,
  In death or life, to be without her there.

If I could see her once again today
  At sunset, see her fawnlike, gracious eyes,
If on her heavenly bosom I could lay
  My cheek and rest — oh, I should quite despise
  The saint, the king, the blest in Paradise.

For I remember fervently today
  Her beauty perfect in its every part,
To which all other lovely women pay
  Their homage, for 'tis far beyond their art—
  Queen of love's drama, mistress of my heart!

I could not, if I would, forget today
  Even for a moment, such a wondrous wife,
So young, so helpless that she seems to pray
  For pity, stabbed by love as by a knife,
  Nearer than garments are, more dear than life.

The vision of her beauty comes today
  To make all other beauty seem awry,
To shame the pride of women, and to slay
  Men's hearts by hundreds; and I know that I,
  Consumed by absent fires, shall surely die.

Heroic wisdom, teach me how today
  To act, to save a life than life more dear,
And deeds of heaven's heroes to outweigh;
  For well I know that death is creeping near,
  And for my bride, my brave, true bride, I fear.

RELATIVES

My bride! And must I think of her today
  With bright eyes dimmed by sorrow and by fears,
With light feet treading slow the future gray;
  I hear her voice come stumblingly through tears,
  And see her bowed by woe through endless years.

For I have never seen, nor see today
  A face that with my darling's could compare,
Though all the rival world should challenge. Nay,
  The sweetness of Love's wife is not so rare;
  The moon itself is not so spotless fair.

Her wealth of wondrous hair I see today,
  Her teeth of pearl; and I remember well
How sorrow in her presence would not stay;
  How union with my bride would ever spell
  The bliss of heaven; one moment's absence, hell.

The last grim moment I recall today
  When from her palace slaves that seemed to be
Resistless slaves of Death, tore me away,
  And all her prayers for me were vain; yet she
  Still gazed and gazed. That gaze still tortures me.

RELATIVES

I think with anguish of her face today—
  The face that in its beauty overbore
The wonder of the moon's unclouded ray—
  Because upon that face I may not pore
  Again, and yet again, and evermore.

I think of her, my hope of life, today,
  How she would listen with her mind and heart
To all I said. My maiden young and gay,
  Thy youth was mine alone, thine artless art,
  And shall be mine again, though death us part.

And I recall what I have lost today
  How she would move in such sweet perfume clad
That bees would gather round her cheek alway;
  The very tinkle that her bracelets had
  When she would fix her hair, will drive me mad.

And I remember woefully today
  How gently I would waken her, while she
Would shiver, and her startled eyes would stray,
  Unable yet our love's new day to see—
  She wakes, starts back, then recognizes me.

And I recall another hour today
  When, jealous, she would leave me. I entreat
Her, and she does not turn her face away
  But weeps when kissed. I fall before her feet:
  "Be gracious to thine humble servant, sweet.

Thou canst not think that I would fall today
  In thy bed-chamber, victim to the glance
Of others, I, the subject of thy sway—
  Far rather would I perish in a trance
  Of thy dear kisses, playfulness, and dance."

I wonder, as I think of her today,
  If she be heaven's queen come down to earth,
Or Shiva's bride, or Vishnu's. Or she may
  Be God's own thought of beauty in mortal birth,
  To drive men mad with woman's perfect worth.

There is no man that lives on earth today
  Who could depict her; none but me has seen
Such beauty. Should the king of heaven essay
  The task, with memories of his heavenly queen,
  He might succeed. None other could, I ween.

And I remember in my cell today
  How she would stop her ears in graceful fun.
No other face like hers is lovely. Yea,
  And if her form blots out beneath the sun
  All other beauty, why, what harm is done?

No doubt her heavenly features keep today
  The pallid splendor of the autumn moon,
And trip the saint on his ascetic way:
  Would I might gain the glory lost so soon,
  And lose no more forever such a boon!

Ah, yes, if I might plunge again today
  Beneath love's waters that so long I miss,
Might save love's lotus-blossom from decay
  And share with her the heaven of a kiss,
  I'd give my life for one such moment's bliss!

Though lovely women walk the world today
  By tens of thousands, there is none so fair
In all that exhibition and display
  With her most perfect beauty to compare—
  This is my consolation, and my care.

As then she floated, so she floats today
  A swan-queen, down the river of my mind
O'er waves that thrill beneath her plumage gay;
  She leaves my admiration far behind,
  And flying dust of blossoms turns me blind.

In sadness I remember her today,
  The daughter of my king, whom love has driven
To me with timid, eager eyes — then say,
  Was she a goddess, or a nymph of heaven,
  Angel, or fairy, to my longings given?

I cannot for an hour forget today
  From dawn until the evening sinks in night
How, sleeping, she would gather beauty; nay,
  Her form seemed slenderer, her breast more white,
  Her gems more radiant yet, by morning's light.

Her golden beauty comes to me today,
  Her slow, coquettish grace, as she would lie
In shamed humility upon her couch, would pray
  For maddening love and kisses. Oh, might I
  Taste that elixir now, I could not die.

RELATIVES

I could not die, might I enjoy today
  That bliss so deep as almost to be woe;
We hardly knew if it were war or play,
  So fiercely did we clasp each other, so
  Fire-hot with passion did our faces glow.

How could I, after that, endure today
  The subtlest fascinations of another?
Far rather would I end my life straightway;
  Come quickly, Death! Come as a kindly brother,
  With one swift act my spark of life to smother.

God Shiva has his poison even today;
  The ocean guards his awful, hidden fire;
The tortoise bears upon his back alway
  The burden of the earth. However dire
  The things they love, they keep what they desire.

THE STRENUOUS LIFE

From the HITOPADESHA

Success the strenuous will reap,
  And not your pensive sinner;
For when the lion fell asleep,
  He had no deer for dinner.

A SINGLE GRAB

From the PANCHATANTRA

Remember that a single grab
Suffices for a fish or crab,
For fool or woman; and 'tis so
For sot, cement, or indigo.

ART IN A PUPIL

From Kalidasa's MALAVIKA

Art in a pupil shows
  The artist doubly well;
The raindrop turns to pearl
  When falling in a shell.

FATALISM

From the HITOPADESHA

What shall not be, will never be;
  What shall be, will be so:
This tonic slays anxiety;
  Taste it, and end your woe.

EXTRAVAGANCE

From Bhartrihari

They cook their grain in beryl kettles
  With fuel of sandal-shoots,
They plough with ploughs of precious metals
  To get the yercum-roots,
They make a hedge of camphor wood
  About the humblest corn,
Unhappy fools! who are not good
  On earth where they were born.

NATURE

From the HITOPADESHA

The habits we acquire are little worth;
The nature that was ours before our birth
Will master us, while yet we live on earth.

YOUR NATURE

From the HITOPADESHA

Your nature is a thing you cannot beat;
It serves as guide in everything you do:
Give a dog all the meat that he can eat,
You can't prevent his gnawing at a shoe.

PREACHING

From BHARTRIHARI

He longs, with twigs from lotus-bowers
  To bind an elephant,
He strives, with softest siris-flowers
  To sever adamant,
He yearns, with honey-drops alone
  To sweeten ocean's taint,
Who hopes, with sugar-coated tone
  To make a rogue a saint.

DEAD-LOVE

From Amaru

In early days, my husband, we
Were one unsevered entity,
And neither of the lovers knew
Were I the dearer half, or you.
Now you are tyrant of my life,
And I am nothing but your wife.
Oh, it was hard as stone for me,
The fruit of life's alluring tree!

HEAVEN ABOVE AND HEAVEN BELOW

From BHARTRIHARI

Oh, dwell by Ganges' holy wave
Where passion's slave his soul may lave;
Or on the bosom of a girl
Where strings of pearl would charm a churl.

THE BAD SON

From the HITOPADESHA

What profits the begetting of a son,
So he be neither good nor wise?
With sightless eyeballs what is to be done?
They ache and yet they are not eyes.

ENTER INTO THY CLOSET

From Bhartrihari

Although thou sink to hell, fly through the air,
  Or flutter o'er the earth and never cease,
Think not, my soul, to find salvation there:
  Remember God at home, who gives thee peace.

TRY AGAIN

From the Mahabharata

Do not despise yourself, my son,
  For early ill-success;
For things that were not, come to be,
  While things that are, grow less.

THE BLESSING OF SILENCE

From the HITOPADESHA

The fool among the wise may shine
A moment, if his dress be fine;
But
One moment, while his mouth is shut.

SIMPLE DEER-HORN

From the MAHABHARATA

I

Young Deer-horn was a pious youth
Devoted to religious truth,
A hermit innocently good
Who grew to manhood in the wood.

His mother left him at his birth;
He only knew one soul on earth,
His austere father; therefore he
Grew up in natural piety.

Now in a kingdom near at hand
No rain had fallen on the land,
Prevented by the magic skill
Of priests the king had treated ill.

An aged priest advised the king:
"Propitiate the clergy; bring
Pure-minded Deer-horn from the wood,
That hermit innocently good.

He dwells in purity afar;
He does not know what women are:
Fetch him, and then the rain will fall;
Of this I have no doubt at all."

The counsel pleased the king; he planned
To entertain the hermit, and
Invited women of the town
To go and bring young Deer-horn down.

But they refused the royal plan,
Fearing to meet a holy man;
At last an aged crone's ambition
Drove her to undertake the mission.

"If you will give me what I ask,"
She said, "I can fulfill the task;
But I require a rich reward
Of gold and gems, my royal lord."

With royal bounty richly laden,
She took her child, a youthful maiden
More known as beautiful than good,
And so departed to the wood.

II

She waited till the coast was clear,
And then she sent her daughter dear
To interview the hermit who
Had never learned what women do.

The maiden found the lad and said:
"I trust your pious life is led
Without offence, and that your food
Of roots and fruits is sweet and good.

I trust your father's heart is blest
With deep religious peace and rest;
For I am hither come to see
Your unpretending piety."

And Deer-horn answered: "Sir, you are
As radiant as a beaming star;
I never saw a man like you;
Then tell me, sir, what shall I do

To make you happy? Here are roots,
Water, a couch of skins, and fruits.
What vows are yours, most holy sage?
Where is your pious hermitage?"

"My hermitage," the maid replied,
"Is three long leagues from here, beside
The river; there I practise now
A fearfully ascetic vow.

For I have sworn that I will greet
Such other hermits as I meet;
And I must clasp and kiss you too —
So my religion bids me do."

She spurned the fruits that he had offered,
And in their stead to him she proffered
Confectionery sweet and good
That she had brought into the wood.

She gave him fragrant garlands too,
And brilliant garments, clean and new;
She offered wine; and while he quaffed,
She played and swayed and danced and laughed.

She played about him with a ball,
And oft coquettishly would fall
Upon his bosom, until he
Took fire from her immodesty.

At last she saw the deed was done,
That she had charmed the hermit's son;
And, gazing o'er her shoulder, fled,
To make her sacrifice, she said.

When she had left him, peace and joy
Departed from the luckless boy;
Sadly he sighed, by love distressed,
An aching void within his breast.

His father, while he sighed, returned,
Whose eyes with fire ascetic burned,
Whose life was one devoted prayer,
Whose nails were overgrown with hair.

When he beheld his son distressed
With eye upturned and heaving breast,
With longing written on his face
And passion in contentment's place,

"What troubles you, my dearest son?"
He asked, "and are your duties done?
Who has been here with you today?"
And Deer-horn answered him straightway.

III

"A hermit youth with hanging hair,
Not short, nor very tall, but fair
And bright as gold, with lotus-eyes,
Some child of heaven, wondrous wise.

He came in beauty like the sun,
Black eyes, sweet voice, his hair undone
And hanging soft, dark, fragrant, and
Encircled by a golden band.

A relic on his neck was seen
That danced like flashing lightnings keen;
Below it, two soft swellings white
That thrilled me with a strange delight.

Large hips he had, but slender waist
Which I could see was close embraced
By a golden belt; I saw it shine
And it was not at all like mine.

And on his ankles something stirred
That jingled like a cooing bird,
While on his wrist there tinkled free
A novel kind of rosary.

And as he moved, the beads would sing
Like gay flamingoes in the spring;
His pious robe was wondrous fair,
And quite unlike the garb we wear.

His face was beautiful to see;
His speech was kind and gladdened me;
His voice was like the nightingale;
It made me sigh and yearn and pale.

And as in spring the forest trees
Wave beautifully in the breeze,
So, father, when the wind blew, he
Shed fragrance like a flowering tree.

His hermit locks—I wondered how
They parted on his noble brow;
And dangling from each ear, there stirred
And danced what seemed a brilliant bird.

A round, elastic fruit he had
That bounded from the earth like mad
When he would strike it merrily—
'Twas very wonderful to see.

He moved and swayed with graceful ease—
I thought of wind among the trees:
A wonderful delight and joy
Came when I saw the godlike boy.

He held me in a tight embrace;
I felt his hair; he pressed his face
Against my face and made a noise
That waked in me the strangest joys.

Our simple fruits he did not think
Were good, or water that we drink;
He gave me other fruits and rare,
And said: 'This is my humble fare.'

They were not like the fruits we eat,
But tasted wonderfully sweet;
They had a different sort of skin,
And different was the pulp within.

A strange, sweet kind of water he
Offered with noble piety;
It filled me with an odd delight,
And earth grew wobbly to my sight.

Sweet garlands with a careless mirth
He wove, and scattered on the earth;
Then, glorious as an ancient sage,
Departed to his hermitage.

And since he went, I feel distressed;
My limbs are burning and my breast;
I long to go to him today
Or have him here with me alway.

Yes, I will tread the path he trod
And learn the way he worships God;
With him I long to make a trial
Of holy life and self-denial.

I find no peace from him apart;
Religious yearnings fill my heart."

IV

"It was a devil, dear my son;
By foes like these we are undone;
They walk the earth in conquering charm
And work religious men much harm.

They win us with their cunning wiles,
Their wondrous beauty and their smiles,
Then show themselves as demons fell
And plunge us in the pit of hell.

The man who seeks religious peace
Should keep himself from such as these;
To ruin us, is their delight,
My pious boy. Forget the sight.

And those sweet waters that you had
Are tasted only by the bad;
And we ascetics never wear
A perfumed garland on our hair.

Resist the devil, boy;'' he said
And then he hunted for the jade;
Three days he sought without success
And ceased for very weariness.

Meantime, the tempting minx returned,
And seeing her, young Deer-horn burned;
"Come quick,'' he said, "and let us roam;
You see my father's not at home.

Your hermitage I fain would view;''
So, hand in eager hand, they flew
And found a boat and floated down
The river to the royal town.

No sooner did the hermit gain
The royal palace than the rain
Fell, drenching every thirsty part
And gladdening the sovereign's heart.

The joyful monarch to the brave,
Bewildered young ascetic gave —
Lest he should ever seek release —
A princess — and her name was Peace.

PEACE

From Bhartrihari

I would not call a friend or foe mine own,
A gem or clod, a bed of flowers or stone,
A serpent or a string of precious pearls,
A bunch of grasses or a bunch of girls,
So might I see with calm, unwavering eye
My peaceful days move softly gliding by,
The while I murmured in a pious grove
To Shiva, Shiva, Shiva, all my love.

VISION

From the HITOPADESHA

Who sees his life in others' life,
 In others' wealth a clod, a weed,
His mother in his neighbor's wife,
 He sees, he sees indeed.

I LOVE THE WOODS

From Bhartrihari

Girl, girl! What mean those tender glances
Like budding flowers in languid dances?
Stop, stop! Your art no more entrances.

I love the woods. My childish madness
Awakens memories of sadness.
The world? A straw brings equal gladness.

NO COMPROMISE

From Kalidasa's Malavika

Oh, I would have her whole,
  Else leave her free;
Not clasp her, while her soul
  Is not for me.

No, let us rather die
  Hopeless, apart,
If in a lonely sigh
  Heart answers heart.

CAUSE AND EFFECT

From Bhartrihari

As knowledge in the just
Increases self-distrust;
In others, pride and lust—

Just so, the saint will find
When lonely, peace of mind;
Not so the lovesick kind.

NATURAL BEAUTY

From Bhartrihari

The color on the lily's face
Is natural. So is maiden grace.
The bee flits vainly round the flower,
The fool round beauty's virgin power.

WOMAN'S WEAPONS

From Bhartrihari

The skilfully coquettish frown,
Bashfulness choking laughter down,
The love-word seeming free from guile,
The undulating step, the smile —
These things, to every woman true,
Are ornaments, and weapons too.

THE FAILURE OF EDUCATION

From Bhartrihari

Uneducated moths will fly
  Into the blazing fire;
Ignorant fish will take the hook
  In the bait of their desire.
And we who know so many things
  Forget the price, and feed
The creeping lusts that coil us round —
  Oh! We are fools indeed.

A NEGLECTED EDUCATION

From the HITOPADESHA

Alas, my foolish, foolish boy,
Whose nights are spent in thoughtless joy,
Among the wise as ill you stand,
As some poor cow in boggy land.

YAYATI'S SONG

From the MAHABHARATA

Desire is never satisfied
  By winning each desire;
As fuel, added to the blaze,
  Gluts not the hungry fire.

Not all the barley in the world
  And rice and gold and kine
And women, are enough for one —
  Remember, and resign.

For when our longings and our sins
  Toward every creature cease,
When deed and thought and word are pure,
  We find eternal peace.

When all things lose their fear of us,
  And when we find release
From fear of them, and hate, and hope,
  We have eternal peace.

GOOD-BYE TO SPRING

From Kalidasa's MALAVIKA

The mango trees are bending
  Beneath the fruits they bring;
The amaranths are spending
  Their flowers with lavish fling;
The heart of youth is sending
  A sad good-bye to spring.

USE THE ROD

From the ANTHOLOGY

The youngsters nowadays run wild
From petting; whipping makes them mild.
  And therefore I would never pet
But whip a pupil or a child.

LITTLE CHILDREN

From Kalidasa's SHAKUNTALA

They show their little buds of teeth
  In peals of causeless laughter;
They hide their trustful heads beneath
  Your heart. And stumbling after

Come sweet, unmeaning sounds that sing
  To you. The father warms
And loves the very dirt they bring
  Upon their little forms.

STRIKE

From the HITOPADESHA

Fear fearful things, while yet
  No fearful thing appears;
When dangers must be met,
  Strike, and forget your fears.

When all his safety lies
  In fighting, blow for blow,
The wise man fights and dies,
  And with him dies his foe.

WHY MEN FIGHT

From Bhartrihari

Perhaps the warrior, smitten by his foe,
Will rise to heaven and leave the world below;
  Perhaps the fighting is its own reward;
No god has told us and we do not know.

We only know that the applauding beat
Of eager hands, the joyous shouts that greet
  The sturdy fighter from his foes and friends,
Are music in his ears, and very sweet.

AFTER LIFE'S FITFUL FEVER

From Bhartrihari

My mind no longer loves philosophy
No longer seeks delight in poetry,
Contemns the paths of doubt so often trod,
And yearns to be united with its God.

THE INTELLIGENT CORPSE

From Bhartrihari

A beggar in the graveyard cried:
"Awake, my friend, be satisfied
To live again and bear the weight
Of poverty; for I of late
Am weary grown; my heart is led
To crave the comfort of the dead."
The corpse was silent; he was sure
'Twas better to be dead than poor.

WISDOM'S SOUP

From the MAHABHARATA

A scholar who can merely quote
Unmastered learning got by rote,
Is erudition's luckless dupe,
A spoon to ladle wisdom's soup.

The fool who hears but cannot prize
The wisdom of the truly wise,
He too is erudition's dupe,
A spoon to ladle wisdom's soup.

But you, dear reader, if you prize
This wisdom of the truly wise,
Will soon be added to the group
Of tongues that relish wisdom's soup.